C'EST À TOI!

Level Three

About the Cover

First Love, the painting on the cover of the third level of *C'est à toi!*, is another original acrylic created expressly for this series by Kelly Stribling Sutherland. Reminiscent of *The Birthday* by the Russian-born French artist Marc Chagall, a man offers a bouquet of flowers to his girlfriend. Swept away with his expression of love, she floats through the air. As your class studies French art in Unit 3, you may want to have them compare this painting with the fantasy done by Chagall. Both portray a moment of celebration with unique imagery, depicting passion with a swirling, upward movement and bright blocks of pure color. The surrealism in *The Birthday* has been made even more whimsical by Ms. Sutherland's addition of two well-known nursery rhyme characters: the cat with the fiddle and the cow jumping over the moon.

REVISED

C'EST À TOI!
Level Three

Annotated Teacher's Edition

Authors

Augusta DeSimone Clark

Richard Ladd

Sarah Vaillancourt

Diana Moen

EMC/Paradigm Publishing, Saint Paul, Minnesota

FL-F
Em23
2002
8
tg

ISBN 0-8219-2260-2

Published by EMC/Paradigm Publishing
875 Montreal Way
St. Paul, Minnesota 55102
800-328-1452
www.emcp.com
E-mail: educate@emcp.com

Printed in the United States of America
1 2 3 4 5 6 7 8 9 10 XXX 07 06 05 04 03 02

Contents

SCOPE AND SEQUENCE CHART

Unité	Leçon	Fonctions	Vocabulaire
1 *La vie scolaire et les passe-temps*	A	inquiring about the past describing past events sequencing events summarizing inquiring about ability expressing inability giving examples confirming a known fact	school subjects school supplies
	B	giving orders explaining something giving examples offering something expressing astonishment and disbelief expressing enthusiasm expressing emotions expressing desire	amusement parks sports
2 *Les rapports humains*	A	asking for information expressing astonishment and disbelief expressing ridicule telling a story describing how things were telling how you were describing physical traits describing temperament	adjectives
	B	writing a letter telling a story explaining something expressing emotions expressing concern expressing suspicion apologizing expressing satisfaction	office workers reflexive verbs

3
Les arts
	A	inquiring about likes and dislikes
		expressing likes and dislikes
		listing
		stating a generalization
		stating a preference
		expressing need and necessity
		inquiring about opinions
		giving opinions
			movies
			art
			expressions dealing with:
			  Daniel Auteuil
			  Marguerite Duras
			  Céline Dion
			  Angélique Kidjo
			  Maurice Jarre
			  Camille Claudel
			  Gustave Caillebotte

	B	asking about importance and unimportance expressing importance and unimportance inquiring about agreement and disagreement giving opinions inquiring about surprise comparing inquiring about possibility and impossibility expressing possibility and impossibility expressing need and necessity telling location	movies entertainment expressions

Enquête culturelle	Structure	Sur la bonne piste
Senegal education in Senegal education in France school supplies	present tense of regular verbs ending in *-er*, *-ir* and *re* present tense of irregular verbs interrogative pronouns direct object pronouns: *me, te, le, la, nous, vous, les* indirect object pronouns: *me, te, lui, nous, vous, leur*	writing a composition
La Ronde in Montreal cafés *le Carnaval* sports in Quebec	*passé composé* with *avoir* *passé composé* with *être* the pronoun *y* the pronoun *en* double object pronouns	review of reading strategies "La plage, c'est chouette" Sempé/Goscinny
passports travel tips *le métro*	imperfect tense present participle	narrating
international travel airports European Union French police Georges Simenon	reflexive verbs negation other negative expressions	creating mental images "Déjeuner du matin" "Le Cancre" Jacques Prévert
TV	the imperfect and the *passé composé* present tense of the irregular verb *plaire* the subjunctive of regular verbs after *il faut que*	explaining in detail
entertainment guides movies	*c'est* vs. *il/elle est* the subjunctive of irregular verbs the subjunctive after impersonal expressions	characterization *Au revoir, les enfants* Louis Malle

Unité	Leçon	Fonctions	Vocabulaire
4 *Le monde du travail*	**A**	writing a letter expressing desire stating want expressing hope stating a preference describing talents and abilities evaluating making requests expressing that you expect a positive response expressing appreciation	adjectives want ads business letters
	B	interviewing giving opinions expressing disagreement explaining a problem inquiring about certainty and uncertainty expressing certainty and uncertainty expressing intentions sequencing events	unemployment

5
Comment se débrouiller en voyage
	A	expressing likes and dislikes
		agreeing and disagreeing
		expressing surprise
		giving opinions
		expressing fear
		inquiring about possibility and
		    impossibility
		controlling the volume of a
		    conversation
		expressing dissatisfaction
		expressing regret
		making requests
		expressing happiness
		telling location
			hotel expressions

	B	writing postcards telling location telling a story remembering describing people you remember indicating knowing and not knowing identifying objects expressing complaint admitting expressing patience	airplane expressions train expressions

Enquête culturelle	Structure	Sur la bonne piste
women in the work force young adults and jobs preparing for a job	*depuis* + present tense the subjunctive after expressions of wish, will or desire	writing a résumé
working conditions workers' benefits unemployment	the relative pronouns *qui* and *que* the relative pronouns *ce qui* and *ce que* the subjunctive after expressions of doubt or uncertainty	deciphering want ads
classifying hotels Saint-Martin	conditional tense the subjunctive after expressions of emotion	telling a story through pictures
Gaspé Peninsula *le Rocher Percé* *le Parc de l'Île-Bonaventure- et-du-Rocher-Percé* American vs. European trains	verbs + *de* + nouns the relative pronoun *dont*	satire *La cantatrice chauve* Eugène Ionesco

Unité	Leçon	Fonctions	Vocabulaire
6 *L'avenir: la technologie et l'environnement*	A	giving information sequencing events listing explaining something giving opinions expressing probability predicting	space technology computers
	B	asking for information giving information sequencing events giving opinions expressing enthusiasm hypothesizing predicting congratulating and commiserating expressing appreciation forgetting making requests	social problems newspaper expressions
7 *Les Français comme ils sont*	A	asking for information stating a generalization explaining something comparing requesting clarification inquiring about opinions expressing surprise inquiring about satisfaction and dissatisfaction proposing solutions	*la cité*
	B	asking about preference stating preference clarifying reporting comparing expressing importance and unimportance agreeing and disagreeing describing character expressing compassion	adjectives

8
L'histoire de France
	A	describing past events
		using links
		sequencing events
		explaining something
		having something done
		describing character
		stating a generalization
		boasting
		expressing appreciation
			expressions dealing with:
			    Vercingétorix
			    Charlemagne
			    Guillaume le Conquérant
			    Louis IX

	B	describing past events
		stating factual information
		sequencing events
		expressing obligation
		expressing incapability
		expressing criticism
		stating a preference
			expressions dealing with:
			    Catherine de Médicis
			    Louis XVI
			    le marquis de La Fayette
			    Georges Haussmann

Enquête culturelle	Structure	Sur la bonne piste
le TGV l'Eurostar l'Agence spatiale européenne le Minitel computers	comparative of adjectives superlative of adjectives future tense	using computer technology
la Fondation Brigitte Bardot Médecins Sans Frontières l'Équipe Cousteau	future tense in sentences with si future tense after quand	figures of speech rhyme scheme "Comme un Arbre" Maxime LeForestier
Togo les HLM les allocations familiales immigrants in France	conditional tense in sentences with si the interrogative adjective quel the interrogative pronoun lequel	circumlocuting
fast-food restaurants French restaurant chains family structure le franglais French department stores	demonstrative adjectives demonstrative pronouns	setting Les petits enfants du siècle Christiane Rochefort
Jules César Astérix Dijon La Chanson de Roland la tapisserie de Bayeux les croisades	expressions with faire faire + infinitive	summarizing a literary selection

Huguenots
Nostradamus
Marie-Antoinette
the French and American
  Revolutions
Benjamin Franklin
Pierre L'Enfant
	expressions with avoir
	past infinitive
		research strategies
		Le Bourgeois gentilhomme
		  Molière

Unité	Leçon	Fonctions	Vocabulaire
9 *L'Afrique francophone*	A	describing past events asking what something is identifying objects telling location reminding expressing indifference expressing disappointment expressing enthusiasm boasting	African wildlife African housing
	B	writing a letter telling a story describing past events sequencing events using links giving information expressing ownership comparing	African game African landscape
10 *On s'adapte*	A	inquiring about health and welfare giving information describing character inquiring about capability asking for help expressing displeasure agreeing and disagreeing comparing accepting and refusing an invitation expressing gratitude terminating a conversation	hospital expressions injuries pharmacy expressions
	B	describing past events asking for permission expressing confirmation admitting asking for a price estimating hypothesizing agreeing and disagreeing expressing emotions expressing disappointment making suggestions	shopping electronic equipment

Enquête culturelle	Structure	Sur la bonne piste
Niger *le musée national de Niamey*	expressions with *être* pluperfect tense	comparing and contrasting
Mali Oumou Sangaré	possessive adjectives possessive pronouns	cultural inferences *Trois Prétendants, un Mari* Guillaume Oyônô-Mbia
Fontainebleau soccer *le SAMU* the Good Samaritan law pharmacies	expressions of quantity indefinite adjectives indefinite pronouns	persuading
le Midi Avignon	past conditional tense past conditional tense in sentences with *si*	reading instructions

Introduction

C'est à toi! is a revised three-level French program that has been developed in response to needs expressed by teachers throughout the country who are looking for the latest in a communication-based, functional approach to teaching French language and culture. Based on detailed surveys involving hundreds of experienced educators and information gleaned from focus groups conducted in various parts of the country, *C'est à toi!* offers an innovative, creative approach to meeting the needs of students in the twenty-first century.

When the *Goals 2000: Educate America Act* provided funding for improving education in 1994, a K-12 Student Standards Task Force was formed to establish content standards in foreign language education. The National Standards in Foreign Language Education Project brought together a wide array of educators, organizations and interested individuals to discuss and establish a new national framework of standards for foreign language education in the United States. The resulting document, titled *Standards for Foreign Language Learning: Preparing for the 21ˢᵗ Century*, provides a bold vision and a powerful framework for understanding language learning. These standards will help shape instruction and assessment for years to come.

The National Standards identify and describe 11 content standards that correspond to the organizing principle of five interconnected Cs: Communication, Cultures, Connections, Comparisons and Communities. The *C'est à toi!* program was specifically designed to address these standards, and they are cross-referenced in the lower left- and lower right-hand corners of the pages of *C'est à toi!*, using the numbering system as it appears in the standards:

Communication

Communicate in Languages Other Than English

Standard 1.1: Students engage in conversations, provide and obtain information, express feelings and emotions and exchange opinions.

Standard 1.2: Students understand and interpret written and spoken language on a variety of topics.

Standard 1.3: Students present information, concepts and ideas to an audience of listeners or readers on a variety of topics.

Cultures

Gain Knowledge and Understanding of Other Cultures

Standard 2.1: Students demonstrate an understanding of the relationship between the practices and perspectives of the culture studied.

Standard 2.2: Students demonstrate an understanding of the relationship between the products and perspectives of the culture studied.

Connections

Connect with Other Disciplines and Acquire Information

Standard 3.1: Students reinforce and further their knowledge of other disciplines through the foreign language.

Standard 3.2: Students acquire information and recognize the distinctive viewpoints that are available only through the foreign language and its cultures.

Comparisons

Develop Insight into the Nature of Language and Culture

Standard 4.1: Students demonstrate understanding of the nature of language through comparisons of the language studied and their own.

Standard 4.2: Students demonstrate understanding of the concept of culture through comparisons of the cultures studied and their own.

Communities

Participate in Multilingual Communities at Home and Around the World

Standard 5.1: Students use the language both within and beyond the school setting.

Standard 5.2: Students show evidence of becoming life-long learners by using the language for personal enjoyment and enrichment.

C'est à toi! features a fresh approach to function-based communication in all three modes: interpersonal, interpretive and presentational. Written by active and experienced high school French teachers who deal daily with students just like yours, the *C'est à toi!* program provides a realistic balance among all five skill areas that will develop proficiency in each one. Paired, small group and cooperative group activities are at the heart of today's student-centered classroom. In the *C'est à toi!* program, students assume a more active role in their learning, working with each other to accomplish linguistic tasks, with teachers serving primarily as facilitators.

The comprehensive *C'est à toi!* program, composed of the textbook and its fully integrated set of additional components, offers instructors and students the most complete materials possible to teach and learn French. The accompanying ancillaries may be used as enrichment, additional practice or reinforcement. These tailor-made materials, which fit individual students' needs and learning styles, include the annotated teacher's edition, annotated teacher's edition on CD-ROM, workbook, assessment program (with quizzes, tests, portfolio assessment with proficiency tests, and test generator on CD-ROM), audiocassette/CD program, teacher's resource kit, program manager (with daily lesson plans), video program, overhead transparencies, Internet activities and Internet resource center. One of the greatest challenges that teachers face today is reaching students with varying abilities, backgrounds, interests and learning styles. The extensive instructional program of *C'est à toi!* recognizes, anticipates and provides for these differences.

About This Annotated Teacher's Edition

The front section of this Annotated Teacher's Edition contains:

- a Scope and Sequence Chart that gives a complete overview of each unit in *C'est à toi!*
- a description of each section of the textbook along with a list of the other *C'est à toi!* components
- relevant information about the program's authors
- philosophy of proficiency, culture, structure and reading
- the *C'est à toi!* program's philosophy and learning strategies that are incorporated in the textbook
- model lesson plans for both regular class periods and block scheduling
- a list of practical classroom expressions (**Expressions de communication**)
- a list of all the communicative functions covered in *C'est à toi!* and the units in which they are first practiced

The annotated version of the expanded student textbook contains:

- correlations of ancillary materials to the textbook

    a. **Workbook Activity**

    b. **Audiocassette/CD Activity**

    c. **Transparency**

    d. **Listening Activity**

    e. **Quiz**

    f. **Advanced Placement**

- correlations of the textbook to the National Standards

NATIONAL STANDARDS

- answers to both oral and written activities (except where answers are personalized)
- cultural notes (information that may be useful to teachers and interesting to students)
- additional background information
- linguistic and pronunciation notes
- teaching suggestions
  a. paired activities
  b. cooperative group practice
  c. TPR
  d. comparisons (critical thinking skills)
  e. connections (cross-curricular activities)
  f. games
  g. activities to engage students' multiple intelligences
  h. ideas for modifying and expanding activities

Components

C'est à toi! is a comprehensive three-level French language program written to meet the needs of French students as they enter the twenty-first century. The third-level program includes the following components:

- Textbook
- Annotated Teacher's Edition
    - Annotated Teacher's Edition on CD-ROM
- Workbook
- Workbook Teacher's Edition
- Teacher's Resource Kit
    - Additional Listening Activities
    - Additional Listening Activities Teacher's Edition
    - Audiocassettes/CDs with Additional Listening Activities
    - Workbook Teacher's Edition
    - Audiocassette/CD Program Manual
    - Program Manager with Daily Lesson Plans
- Audiocassette/CD Program
    - Audiocassettes/CDs
    - Audiocassette/CD Program Manual
- Assessment Program
    - Lesson Quizzes
    - Lesson Quizzes Teacher's Edition
    - Unit Tests Booklet
    - Unit Tests Booklet Teacher's Edition
    - Unit Tests Audiocassettes/CDs
    - Portfolio Assessment with Proficiency Tests
    - Test Generator on CD-ROM
- Video Program
    - Videos
    - Video Manual
- Overhead Transparencies
- Internet Activities
- Internet Resource Center

Textbook

This revised textbook contains 10 **unités**. Each **unité** is composed of two **leçons**, labeled **A** and **B**. At the end of the textbook you will find a grammar summary, an end vocabulary section (French/English and English/French) and a grammar index. All the **unités** have been designed in a similar manner so that students will be familiar with the format and know exactly what to expect. Each lesson gives students the communicative functions, vocabulary, structures and cultural information necessary to communicate in authentic French about a variety of everyday situations that interest teenagers. The entire textbook's active vocabulary is less than 900 words, and grammatical structures are recycled systematically to help students bridge from the known to the unknown.

Unit Opener — The unit begins with a list of communicative functions. This provides a preview of the tasks that students will be able to accomplish when they complete the unit. Functions are continually recycled from one unit to the next, with functions repeated only when a different way of expressing that specific function is introduced. A two-page photo or collage visually prepares students for one of the main cultural components of the unit.

Lesson Opener — Each lesson begins with a list of the communicative functions that pertain to that lesson. Next come colorful illustrations or photos that introduce all the new vocabulary groups and expressions in the lesson in a meaningful context. Students should be told that illustrations and photos in the lesson opener are part of the basic textbook material, visually explaining words and expressions that students are expected to know.

Tes empreintes ici — This section, new in the third-level textbook, follows the list of communicative functions in **Leçon A**. It offers introductory, personalized questions intended to motivate students and connect them with the unit's topic(s). This section encourages students to compare and contrast their experiences with those they will read about.

Dossier ouvert — Also new in the third-level textbook, this section presents a cultural "teaser" to challenge students to interact and problem solve in an authentic cultural situation in the francophone world. Students answer a multiple-choice question about how they would react in the given situation. (Its answer and explanation are given in the **Dossier fermé** section at the end of the unit.)

Dialogue — Next comes a dialogue, letter, postcard, journal entry or reading that follows a natural format and dramatizes a situation typical of everyday life in francophone regions. Speakers represent a cross section of age groups, although the emphasis is on activities of teenagers. The exposition is introduced with a colorful illustration that reinforces the cultural content and makes each situation more meaningful. The exposition contains an example of how each one of the lesson's communicative functions is expressed. (This is summarized for students in the **Communication active** section in the **C'est à moi!** review section at the end of every unit.) Each exposition has been carefully designed not only to present authentic speech but also to contain at least one instance in which each of the new structures in the lesson is used. All words in the exposition are active vocabulary; that is, students are expected to produce the words in **Pratique** and **Communication** activities and use them again in following units. To understand the lesson's new vocabulary words, students can look back at the introductory illustrations, refer to the glossary following the exposition or infer meaning from the context. Previously learned words and structures are regularly recycled.

Activités — Following the exposition is a series of activities that checks comprehension of its content and new vocabulary that has been presented either visually or in context. Following the comprehension activities, students are challenged to answer personalized questions dealing with the exposition's theme in the **C'est à toi!** activity. All of these activities may be done orally, in writing or both.

Enquête culturelle — Directly after the ***Activités***, a group of notes highlights certain cultural subtleties or presents more detailed information about the French-speaking world. These notes are not related to each other; they refer to various sentences in the exposition and expand on the information presented there. These comments are intended to heighten students' interest in, appreciation for and understanding of certain aspects of francophone culture and to provide insight into the daily activities of French speakers. Accompanying photos help to expand students' cultural horizons. Comprehension questions and realia-based activities help students apply what they have learned.

Journal personnel — This is another new section in the third-level textbook. Students record their observations about specific aspects of francophone culture, note similarities and differences between it and their own and reflectively compare them, writing either in French or English.

Structure — This section presents the lesson's main grammatical topics in a concise, clear manner. Examples in French are presented along with their English equivalents to help students' comprehension. Colorful charts provide reinforcement as do photo captions that illustrate how the specific structures are used in context.

Pratique — Following the presentation of each grammar topic is the **Pratique** section, composed of contextualized activities that allow students to practice both oral and written skills. Realistic situations as a basis for the activities make students' communication more relevant. You may choose whether students respond orally, in writing or both. The more mechanical activities precede those that allow students more creativity or are open-ended. The type of activities in the **Pratique** section varies— those based on visual cues and realia, dehydrated sentences, paired activities and sentence completion. The **Modèle**, in the side margin, demonstrates a correct response to help students succeed immediately.

Communication — A group of proficiency-based activities appears at the end of each lesson following the last **Structure** and **Pratique** sections. These activities provide opportunities for students to develop oral and written proficiency using the functions that are presented in each lesson. Task-based paired and cooperative learning activities as well as activities that encourage the development of multiple intelligences foster the creative use of French to practice using the lesson's vocabulary and structures to express specific functions. For example, students may be asked to write lists, design invitations and menus, order at a restaurant, conduct surveys and interviews, label photos, do role-plays, write postcards and faxes, make posters and drawings, give directions or review films.

Sur la bonne piste — There are two **Sur la bonne piste** sections in each unit of the third-level textbook. They highlight various reading, writing and oral communication strategies in French. Techniques for successfully completing tasks associated with college placement exams are also included. The section in **Leçon A** focuses on strategies for successful function-based oral and written communication. For example, students learn how to write compositions and résumés, circumlocute and tell stories using visual cues. The section in **Leçon B** features specific strategies appropriate to third-level reading selections. Each unit focuses on a different literary technique to help students experience success as they read in French. Students are carefully guided before and as they read authentic French texts (stories, poems, excerpts from plays, screenplays and novels) so that they can apply the strategies presented in each unit. Various activities follow, some calling for specific answers and others calling for critical thinking and interpretation. The Annotated Teacher's Edition gives suggestions on how to holistically grade these answers.

Dossier fermé — Students "uncover" the answer and explanation to the cultural "teaser" presented earlier in the **Dossier ouvert** section.

C'est à moi! — The first of the seven-part review section at the end of each unit, **C'est à moi!** consists of a personalized checklist of all the functions that have been introduced in the unit. If students are unsure of how to express a certain function, they should look for an example of it in the following **Communication active** section. **C'est à moi!** also has a true-false quiz on the cultural information presented in the unit's **Enquêtes culturelles**.

Communication orale — This cumulative oral proficiency activity usually takes the form of a paired role-play. Students are carefully guided as to what each partner should include in the conversation. The activity combines all the elements in the unit — functions, topics, vocabulary and structures — into one final, contextualized situation.

Communication écrite — This cumulative proficiency-based writing activity is the written equivalent of the **Communication orale**. Again, students are carefully guided as to what they should include in their postcards, journal entries, reports, letters and newspaper articles.

Communication active — The fifth part of the review section summarizes all of the unit's communicative functions. Along with each function are the phrases used in the unit to express each language task. English equivalents are also given for easy reference. The words in boldface type are the invariable elements; those not in bold may change depending on the specific information that students want to express.

Communication électronique — This new technology section features an exploratory Internet activity correlated specifically to the cultural content of the unit. Students are directed to a Web site, given careful directions on how to proceed and then asked questions about what they have discovered. These questions range from those that check content to more open-ended, discovery questions. Students practice their language skills in French as they explore authentic realia and read up-to-the-minute information about francophone culture. (Note that the Internet is a fast-paced technology, and Web pages and Web addresses are constantly changing or disappearing. You may need to substitute different addresses from the ones given in the **Communication électronique** throughout the textbook.)

À moi de jouer! — In this new cumulative writing section, students have the chance to show what they can do by putting together everything they have learned so far. Illustrations give students a visual clue as to what they should include in writing their dialogues or descriptive narratives based on the functions and vocabulary in the unit. Students' writing will tend to be more open-ended and creative than in the **Communication écrite** section.

Vocabulaire — The final part of the review section is a list of all the new active words and expressions (with English equivalents) that are introduced in the unit.

Grammar Summary (end of the textbook) — This useful reference section summarizes for students' convenience the structures introduced in all three levels of *C'est à toi!* Present tense forms of all irregular verbs are also included.

Vocabulary (end of the textbook) — All words and expressions introduced as active vocabulary in all three levels of *C'est à toi!* appear in this end vocabulary. The number following the meaning of each word or expression indicates the unit in which it appears for the first time in this book. For convenient and flexible use, both French-English and English-French vocabularies are included. Passive vocabulary found in the direction lines to activities and in authentic readings is not included.

Grammar Index (end of the textbook) — A complete index of the grammar points covered in the third level of *C'est à toi!* is provided for easy reference and location.

Annotated Teacher's Edition

This Annotated Teacher's Edition contains a front section and an annotated version of the student textbook.

Front Section:
- Scope and Sequence Chart
- description of all the program's components
- information about the authors
- philosophy of proficiency, culture, structure and reading
- program philosophy and learning strategies
- model lesson plans (regular and block scheduling)
- classroom expressions
- communicative functions

Annotated Version of the Student Textbook:
- correlations of ancillary materials to the textbook
- correlations of the textbook to the National Standards
- answers to both oral and written activities
- cultural notes
- additional background information
- linguistic and pronunciation notes
- teaching suggestions (paired activities, cooperative group practice, TPR, comparisons (critical thinking skills), connections (cross-curricular activities), activities to engage students' multiple intelligences, games)

Annotated Teacher's Edition on CD-ROM

The annotated version of the student textbook is available on CD-ROM for convenient access to the book. Each page can be viewed on screen and printed out so that teachers don't have to carry the textbook home to plan their classes. Teachers can also click on each of the icons to view and print out pages of the supplementary materials that support each page of the textbook.

Workbook

The workbook reviews and expands on the material covered in the textbook with additional written exercises that reinforce students' language skills and cultural awareness. These innovative activities help students become proficient in written French as they further practice the functions, vocabulary and structures in each unit. The workbook also recombines previously learned language concepts to broaden students' understanding. Again, many of these activities are written situationally to make them more realistic and relevant to students. Realia-based activities prepare students to use French in authentic situations. Exercises in the workbook are carefully coordinated with the textbook. The Annotated Teacher's Edition contains icons that tell where each workbook activity best fits in.

Workbook Teacher's Edition

An answer key for all exercises contained in the workbook is available.

Teacher's Resource Kit

The Teacher's Resource Kit contains a variety of useful and practical tools to help teachers make their daily lesson plans. The following components are included in the Teacher's Resource Kit:

- **Additional Listening Activities (on blackline duplicating masters)**

  There are three additional listening comprehension activities in each unit, one for each lesson and a cumulative dialogue. They check students' ability to understand authentic French speech in the form of narratives or conversations. Students have an answer sheet on which they respond in writing either by completing a checklist or by answering true-false, multiple-choice or matching questions. These activities help to prepare students for the listening comprehension sections of the Unit Tests in the Assessment Program. The Annotated Teacher's Edition contains icons that tell where each listening activity best fits in.

- **Additional Listening Activities Teacher's Edition**

  The complete text for the recorded additional listening activities as well as an answer key is available.

- **Audiocassettes/CDs with Additional Listening Activities**

  These audiocassettes/CDs contain the additional listening activities for each unit.

- **Workbook Teacher's Edition**

  An answer key for all exercises contained in the workbook is available.

- **Audiocassette/CD Program Manual**

  This manual contains the complete script of the recorded material (introduction of new words and expressions, **Dialogue**, **Pratique** and **Sur la bonne piste** sections) for each lesson in the textbook.

- **Program Manager with Daily Lesson Plans**

  The Program Manager pulls together the textbook and all the ancillary materials with daily lesson plans for organizing, preparing and teaching the *C'est à toi!* program. Each day's lesson plan presents the core material from the textbook in the left-hand column. In the right-hand column, across from each core element, are the specific ancillary materials that are appropriate for expansion. There are separate lesson plans for both traditional 45- to 55-minute class periods as well as for classes on the block scheduling system.

Audiocassette/CD Program

The various components included in the Audiocassette/CD Program are:

- **Audiocassettes/CDs**

  The Audiocassette/CD Program is an integral part of *C'est à toi!* Appropriate icons in the Annotated Teacher's Edition designate which material in the textbook has been recorded on cassettes or CDs by native speakers of all ages from a variety of francophone countries. Recorded material in each unit includes:

Introduction of new words and expressions (for student repetition)
Dialogue (recorded as a listening experience)
Pratique (selected activities for student response)
Sur la bonne piste (recorded as a listening experience)

- **Audiocassette/CD Program Manual**

This manual contains the complete script of the recorded material (introduction of new words and expressions, **Dialogue**, **Pratique** and **Sur la bonne piste** sections) for each lesson in the textbook.

Assessment Program

The *C'est à toi!* Assessment Program contains the following components:

- **Lesson Quizzes**

There are two quizzes for each unit, one at the end of every lesson. Each quiz consists of four sections: speaking (role-playing activities or personalized questions), vocabulary, grammar (both mastery and proficiency activities) and culture. These quizzes provide students with excellent practice before they take the unit test. Appropriate icons in the Annotated Teacher's Edition designate at what point in the lesson the quiz may be given.

- **Lesson Quizzes Teacher's Edition**

A complete answer key for the Lesson Quizzes is available.

- **Unit Tests Booklet**

The Unit Tests in the *C'est à toi!* program evaluate to what degree students are attaining the program's goals and objectives. A unique format in assessment allows teachers to design tests that evaluate what they have taught in the way they have taught it. Teachers may choose to use whatever sections reflect their students' learning styles and their teaching style: vocabulary, structure, proficiency writing, culture, listening, speaking and reading. For example, to evaluate students' speaking ability, teachers can choose a paired activity or a teacher/student interview.

- **Unit Tests Booklet Teacher's Edition**

The Teacher's Edition of the Unit Tests Booklet contains the text of the material recorded for the listening comprehension section and answer keys to the listening comprehension section and written sections (vocabulary, structure, proficiency writing, culture, speaking and reading) of each Unit Test.

- **Unit Tests Audiocassettes/CDs**

The Unit Tests Audiocassettes/CDs evaluate students' listening comprehension. Students hear authentic French in conversations or narratives and respond by choosing the best answer or continuation to the conversation. They may also see a visual and respond by choosing the best answer to a related question.

- **Portfolio Assessment with Proficiency Tests**

  The first section of the *C'est à toi!* Portfolio Assessment is a rationale for using portfolios in the French class and tips on how to implement this form of evaluation. Next comes a variety of forms for both students and teachers to complete, such as a learner profile, peer evaluation sheet, communicative functions checklist and suggested rubrics for evaluating oral and written production. The final section contains a proficiency-based exam evaluating all five skills for use at the end of the first semester, and another for use at the end of the year.

- **Test Generator on CD-ROM**

  The IBM- and Macintosh-compatible test generator allows teachers to test exactly as they have taught, allowing for differences in instructional emphases, teaching approaches and students' learning styles. Teachers can select and modify sections from the existing Assessment Program, including Units Tests, Lesson Quizzes and Proficiency Tests, in order to create and print their own customized tests. The CD also allows teachers to add their own test questions as well as edit existing questions.

Video Program

The various components included in the Video Program are:

- **Videos**

  As its name suggests, "Trois minutes, s'il vous plaît," the video program coordinated with the third-level textbook, contains 20 short episodes each about three minutes long. Using professional actors and a clever, amusing concept, the video series helps students expand on and review basic vocabulary, structures and functions as they see and hear situations related to themes in the textbook. A subtitled version in French follows each episode. The segments include:

  - *La famille* — A young woman, who is about to be married, has a father who paints family portraits. She shows them to her fiancé, who is not impressed.
  - *Bonjour* — A man and woman, both strangers waiting for a bus, communicate by cell phone.
  - *Au café* — A man and woman meet by chance at a café, and she leaves without paying her bill.
  - *Les vêtements* — As a girl gets ready to go to a party, her father and boyfriend comment on what she is wearing.
  - *En boîte* — Two young adults meet at a disco and start dancing together.
  - *Rendez-vous* — A young man is looking at the personal ads on the Minitel. He arranges to meet a girl, but is she really the one who placed the ad?
  - *À l'hôtel* — The night desk clerk at a hotel has a famous, unexpected guest. Is he dreaming?
  - *Entre amis* — A man starts up a conversation with a woman about the guests at the party they are at. But he doesn't know that she's the hostess.
  - *Ça ne va pas?* — A boy is sick, must stay in bed and can't go out with his girlfriend. He doesn't know that she is sick as well.
  - *Au boulot* — When a father returns home from work, he tells his family that he has just been laid off. His son comes home with news, too.
  - *En vacances* — On vacation in Normandy, a girl complains to her father about the bad weather. But the arrival of a new boy changes her mind.
  - *En voyage* — A briefcase mix-up at a hotel leads to unexpected consequences.

- *À la télé* — A young couple discusses TV programs and has differing opinions on what to watch.
- *Le protagoniste* — A TV performer talks to his makeup artist as she gets him ready for his show.
- *C'est où?* — A participant in the Tour de France has lost his way. Spectators try to help by giving him directions.
- *À la campagne* — A Parisian can't cope with life in the country when he goes to visit relatives.
- *Quelle vie!* — An exhausted wife comes home to find her husband glued to the TV and not about to help her with the housework. Upon waking from a nap, she wonders if her dream has come true.
- *Le gros lot* — A store owner is notified that his shop has sold the winning lotto ticket. But who bought the ticket?
- *Le bal masqué* — Because her husband has to work, a woman goes to an elegant dance alone and meets a charming gentleman.
- *Aux voleurs!* — Two thieves think they have been successful in their attempt at robbery, but they are interrupted by a surprise phone call.

- **Video Manual**

  The Video Manual is included in the Video Program. It contains transcripts of the video units as well as a variety of innovative viewing and post-viewing activities, some based on additional authentic materials.

Overhead Transparencies

A set of 32 full-color transparencies offers illustrations of scenes (as a stimulus for conversation), objects (with identifying overlays), realia, fine art and maps. These transparencies provide an outstanding method of teaching, visually reinforcing or reviewing the lesson's content in a creative, communicative manner. Students can apply their knowledge of vocabulary and culture using different visual stimuli. The Annotated Teacher's Edition contains icons that tell where each transparency best fits in.

Internet Activities

The *C'est à toi!* Internet Activity Web site features contemporary, interesting Internet activities. There are three activities correlated to each unit in the textbook. These Internet activities enhance students' language skills and cultural knowledge as well as develop their Internet research skills. Students are carefully guided through the various links in each activity. Teachers receive a password to allow them to access all the activities' answers. Since the Internet is a changing medium, activities are constantly being added, deleted and modified. To view these activities, visit **www.emcp.com/cestatoi**/.

Internet Resource Center

Internet activities and answers, self quizzes, review exercises and Web links, all coordinated with the units of the *C'est à toi!* textbook, can be found on the Internet Resource Center, accessible from **www.emcp.com**. The site also features general resources for teachers and students, including useful Web links, teaching tips and study aids. The content of the Internet Resource Center is continually being updated.

About the Authors

Augusta DeSimone Clark has been an instructor for 20 years. She teaches French I through French Advanced Placement Language at Saint Mary's Hall in San Antonio, Texas. Clark received her M.A. degree in French Literature from the University of California, Davis. She was selected to be included in *Who's Who Among America's Teachers*, was the recipient of a Holt-DuPont Foundation grant to study and travel in France and received the Outstanding Teacher Award from the University of Chicago. A reader for the College Board, she has also been vice president of the Alliance Française in San Antonio. Clark has served as a mentor to local teachers working to establish French language or AP programs in their schools and has led many student groups on trips to France.

Richard Ladd is an instructor of French and Spanish at Ipswich High School in Ipswich, Massachusetts, where he is department director. He has also taught at various secondary schools and colleges in Massachusetts. Ladd earned his M.A. degree in French from l'École Française, Middlebury College, and a Doctor of Arts in Foreign Language Education from the State University of New York at Stony Brook. A past president of the Massachusetts Foreign Language Association, he has given presentations at local, state, regional and national conferences on a variety of topics, including teaching advanced placement classes, adapting lessons to the long block schedule, using children's literature in the secondary classroom and teaching multilevel classes. Ladd has written video activities booklets and assessment programs for the French classroom. Ladd coauthored *AP French: Preparing for the Language Examination*.

Sarah Vaillancourt is French Editor at EMC/Paradigm Publishing. She is a graduate of Macalester College and the recipient of two NDEA Foreign Language Institute grants, studying in Paris, Tours and Grenoble. She taught French I-V at East High School in Madison, Wisconsin, for 22 years where she received the Bassett Award for Excellence in Teaching. As a program administrator for various student travel organizations, she has taken high school students on more than 20 study-travel tours to Europe, Africa and Canada. Vaillancourt authored the textbooks in the series *Perspectives françaises*, and has been the editor of the textbooks and ancillary materials in the series *Le français vivant* and *C'est à toi!* She has spoken at many state, regional and national foreign language conventions and workshops on topics such as using paired activities for proficiency, engaging students' multiple intelligences and weaving culture through the French curriculum.

Diana Moen is Associate French Editor at EMC/Paradigm Publishing. She received her M.Ed. degree in Second Languages and Cultures from the University of Minnesota. Moen has taught French and English for 15 years in Minnesota high schools and has led student groups to France and Switzerland. She is listed in *Who's Who in the Midwest* and *Who's Who Among America's Teachers*. Moen has been awarded scholarships to study French language and francophone culture in Avignon through the American Association of Teachers of French and in Quebec through the French-Canadian Institute for Language and Culture. She has also received a Rockefeller Fellowship. As a presenter at various regional foreign language conferences, she has shared strategies for teaching the culture of French business that she developed after having completed a seminar at the École Supérieure de Commerce de Lyon.

Foreign Language Proficiency

by Toni Theisen

Proficiency as an organizing concept and as a thoughtful philosophy for second language acquisition has given our content area new life and meaning since its realization in the 1980s with the advent of the ACTFL Proficiency Guidelines. We as language instructors and facilitators are becoming more and more aware of the power, meaning and relevancy of knowing a second language. It is an exciting time to be a part of the profession as we begin to see enrollments increase steadily. We are also encouraged by the growing number of people who value communication skills in our global society. Therefore, the *C'est à toi!* program provides a series of proficiency activities in which students can experience situations in a range of contexts that they would most likely encounter in the francophone culture. Language learners actually use French to solve language tasks.

The ACTFL Proficiency Guidelines

The ACTFL Proficiency Guidelines have given us a clearer definition of the manner and degree in which language is acquired at different levels. We now know the appropriate language tasks and the level of accuracy we can expect from our students in all language skills, ranging from novice-low to superior levels. Proficiency activities involve all language modalities—from listening and reading to speaking and writing, with culture naturally integrated into each language task. We expect novice-mid language learners to function only with limited accuracy in simple survival situations using vocabulary that deals with high-frequency phrases. For example, novice-mid students can successfully order in a café or listen to a set of directions to arrive at a given place. Language learners at the advanced level are able to function at a higher degree of accuracy in situations with a problem or twist, often using circumlocution to negotiate meaning. For example, advanced students are able to write a narrative describing a situation that occurred in the past, such as retelling the events of an accident that they might have witnessed and then relating their reaction to the situation. These guidelines help us design realistic and attainable goals for our language learners.

The Rationale for Proficiency Activities

In order for students to truly own a language, they need to be able to interact with it on successful terms. Proficiency activities act as a catalyst for authentic language use, and students begin to identify with the real purpose of language learning. This ability to interact with others using any of the skills of listening, speaking, reading and writing, all integrated with culture, gives language learners a true sense of accomplishment in French.

Research shows that the optimum scenario for learning is actually doing or experiencing. Through lecture and passive reception, students retain only about 10 percent of the material, whereas with experiential, active learning, students can achieve a 90 percent retention rate. Learning through experience involves students in such a way that vocabulary, structures and functions are put into long-term memory.

Responsibilities of the Learner and Teacher

When incorporating proficiency activities into a lesson, the instructor or facilitator turns over the responsibility of the cognitive learning process to the language learners. It is this opportunity to create with the language that motivates students not only to successfully complete the task, but also to do it with a certain amount of risk involved. As teachers, it is then a part of our job to encourage and effectively praise our students for taking that risk with their acquired language skills and cultural knowledge. In this process, students will discover more ways to negotiate meaning in French. They will arrive at a clear understanding of the linguistic task and all its variables.

Proficiency is a philosophy and not a strategy. Using proficiency as an organizing principle opens the doors to many new learning strategies. This is a great forum for the use of cooperative learning activities that encourage language learners to work together to complete a given task and to depend on and trust each other in order for the group to be successful. The use of pairs and cooperative groups has proved to be tremendously effective in foreign language classrooms. Proficiency also encourages student-centered activities in which the teacher becomes the facilitator of the language. Many instructors integrate authentic materials into their lesson plans as ways to more easily negotiate meaning. Using authentic materials, teachers have learned to change the task rather than change the text.

Proficiency links the learner with language. This real-world use of language framed in real-life situations makes learning French even more relevant. As students strive for higher and higher levels of proficiency, our country will feel more a part of the whole world. In the words of the French Canadian singer Michel Rivard, "C'est la langue de mon cœur et le cœur de ma vie." Hopefully, our students will also feel this way about French.

The Teaching of Culture
by Karla Winther Fawbush

It is impossible to understand another culture thoroughly without speaking its language. Language and culture are directly linked to each other. Words themselves have cultural connotations. For example, the word **marché** evokes an image of a bustling marketplace, the scent of flowers and spices in the air, people bumping into one another as they shop for the freshest produce and the shouts of vendors advertising their wares. What does this say about the value of fresh food in French-speaking households? How do the colors, smells and animation of the marketplace compare to the efficient, sterile atmosphere of the contemporary supermarkets that are springing up in many francophone countries? In what ways does the visual image of the word **marché** help students to understand the deeper aspects of both traditional and contemporary francophone culture?

Ask most students what picture comes to mind when they think of Paris, and they will usually respond "the Eiffel Tower." Built for the World's Fair in 1889, this famous landmark certainly represents the traditional view of French culture: Paris as the center for the best in art, literature, music and architecture. Although historically valid to a point, this definition of culture must be expanded. Culture is more than the great masterpieces of one city; it is how a variety of francophone people speak and behave in everyday situations.

Communicative competency includes both linguistic and cultural proficiency. Therefore, the teaching of culture must extend to every aspect of instruction in a proficiency-based classroom. Certainly there remains a place for the formal, "big C" study of the fine arts in French civilization. Students of all levels of French can appreciate the paintings of Monet, the poems of Prévert, the music of Debussy and the stained glass windows and flying buttresses of Chartres Cathedral. However, the definition of culture needs to extend to a more anthropological view of daily life and language in the francophone world. Why is it inappropriate to bring chrysanthemums as a gift to a dinner party in France? Why should the expression **je suis pleine** be avoided when you have had enough to eat? Why might a young person in Cameroon refer to an adult as Mama Renée or Papa Jean?

Cultural instruction should: (1) expand the study of isolated facts to include a deeper understanding of the various values, beliefs and behavior of French speakers; (2) recognize similarities, as well as differences, among cultures; (3) help students to develop critical thinking skills so that they learn to notice details and work toward independence in novel social situations; and (4) be entwined with the language as a means of communication.

French teachers cannot be expected to be the authority on every aspect of francophone culture. Native guest speakers or teaching assistants, radio and television programs, magazines, newspapers, computer networks, videos and other forms of realia are helpful sources of cultural information.

Moving from the identification of the various components of a cultural program to its implementation in the classroom can be done in several ways. In order to integrate culture into the study of the French language, students should be encouraged to: (1) keep a cultural notebook and make culture a component of their language portfolio; (2) reflect on their own cultural background; and (3) practice questioning and hypothesizing in order to recognize patterns that will help them interact successfully in the francophone culture. Culture engages the heart, and students are most motivated to learn French when it is taught through relevant, meaningful content.

From their first day of French, students should learn to integrate cultural information with the study of the language. By maintaining a cultural notebook, students can explore their own cultural self-awareness as they expand their appreciation of other cultures, learn to express what they have observed, examine their attitudes and enhance their ability to make choices.

As they become exposed to various aspects of francophone culture, students need to examine their own background. For example, students can form groups to select ten items for a time capsule that would represent American culture. Or, students can compare French and American TV commercials to identify the methods used to sell various products in the two cultures. What do these methods say about the subjective values, beliefs and behavior of these two groups? To what extent are the goals (i.e., the need for food, shelter, clothing and education) the same in both cultures?

Students also need to utilize critical thinking skills in order to identify patterns and act appropriately in novel situations. For example, after listening to a foreign exchange student from France, American students may observe that French teenagers seem to rely on automobiles less than they do. Why? At what age do young people in various countries get their driver's license? Is gas more expensive in French-speaking countries than in the United States? Do French-speaking high school students have part-time jobs that would help them pay for the expenses of driving a car? What is public transportation like in francophone countries? Do people often walk or bike to their destination? Finding out the answers to these questions will help students learn to understand francophone culture, while realizing how much of their personal behavior stems from their own geographical and socioeconomic background.

In *C'est à toi!* culture is integrated into the study of French. Dialogues are placed in a variety of francophone settings, as a backdrop for the language itself. Cultural information corresponds to the topics and vocabulary introduced in each unit. Realia engages students to use both inductive and deductive reasoning. Teacher's notes offer supplementary cultural information and suggestions on how to make culture an integral part of each day's activities. For example, in the comparisons activities (critical thinking), questions are provided that students might think about and answer in their cultural journals. Organized on the premise that awakening student interest in the diverse aspects of the francophone world can only enhance linguistic growth, *C'est à toi!* encourages students to widen their cultural horizons as they develop their proficiency in French.

Structural Practice

by Dianne Hopen

Achievement = Personal Experience and Ability + Practice

Each student is the sum of his or her previous learning through a variety of educationally and noneducationally oriented situations, plus his or her ability to process new learning. Student achievement depends on the *amount of practice* available to the student in order to compensate for differing amounts of previous learning and the student's natural ability to learn.

Each of our students enters the language learning setting with a unique set of personal experiences and a differing ability to participate successfully in each new learning situation. As teachers we cannot change our students' previous experience, nor can we alter their ability to learn. What we can do is provide adequate practice.

Research on cognitive learning style preferences has validated foreign language educators' long-held belief that a variety of learning activities is necessary for students to realize their objectives in language learning. Activities that provide contextually meaningful practice are appropriate for all students. Those students with a structured approach to learning benefit the most from structured practice, but all students increase their level of confidence with such practice.

Controlled structural practice or the practice of the mechanics of a language in a contextually meaningful activity allows students to master communicative patterns that lead to the development of free-flowing speech. Students are not logically capable of responding appropriately or accurately in all language settings until they have had the opportunity to practice the functions and vocabulary relating to each particular setting.

Each time a student miscommunicates, it reinforces the importance of accuracy and serves to motivate the student to practice the structure of the language. In a learning setting where both the teacher and the student seek quality control of French for accurate communication, mechanical practice serves as one of the building blocks to success.

Identifying appropriate language components and providing varied and sufficient practice with each one is the goal of the **Structure** sections in the *C'est à toi!* program. Once students have had the opportunity to experience authentic French in realistic situations, structured practice becomes meaningful by providing increasingly more thoughtful practice with manageable portions of communication. This is how students work toward achieving their goal of communicating in French.

Reading

by Linda Klohs

Reasons for Reading

We read for two basic reasons: (1) for pleasure, and (2) for information. In order to read for pleasure, we must first understand what we are reading, that is, read for information. There are various strategies that our students can use to efficiently glean appropriate information from what they read. Unfortunately, these strategies do not come easily to many of them. It is part of our job as educators to find and teach these methods, techniques or strategies.

Learning to Infer: Part of the Reading Act

Many students believe that they must understand each word of every sentence in order to proceed to the next one. In many real-life reading acts, this need to understand each word is not necessary. Furthermore, such dependence is self-defeating, culminating in students' reluctance or refusal to continue when they encounter new or forgotten information or structures. Students need to be encouraged to read for the main idea and to infer meaning from previous sentences or paragraphs or ones that follow.

The Role of the Student and Teacher in the Reading Process

At one time, reading was called a "passive" skill. Many still refer to it as a "receptive" skill. But it is important for students to know that reading is, in fact, an "active" skill. Students must take an active part in the reading process, constantly inferring, deducing, anticipating, guessing, predicting, checking and asking themselves questions about the text. How we, as teachers, encourage them in this process requires us to ask a broader range of questions and accept a wider range of responses than those required by traditional multiple-choice or fill-in-the-blank tests.

Reading Progression in *C'est à toi!*

Readings in the third level of *C'est à toi!* come from original texts that are followed by achievable tasks, such as responding to content questions about an article or recognizing literary devices and interpreting poetry. The difficulty of a reading passage in authentic French depends greatly on what is required of the student after reading the text.

Assessment of the Reading Process

Students bring various personal experiences from life and past reading, both in English and in French, to the reading task. The temptation to lead students toward a single interpretation may curtail thought and enjoyment of a reading passage. If they believe that there is only one answer or way to perceive the reading, many will be discouraged from developing idiosyncratic thought or offering well-thought-out answers. Depending on their level of reading proficiency, students may arrive at various acceptable answers to the activities that follow some of the readings in *C'est à toi!* If students believe that delving deeper into a reading will result in a superior score, many will take the risk to do so. Assessment of students' answers or responses should be judged on a holistic basis, with superior scores given to students who produce more creative or thought-provoking answers. While holistic grading is new to some teachers, suggestions on how to implement this means of assessment are made in the Annotated Teacher's Edition.

Some students depend entirely on teachers for assessment and approval of their work. It becomes increasingly important that as students become more proficient in French, they must be able to diagnose both their own learning process and achievement in the language in order to become independent learners. Teachers can decide when students are ready to self-assess, and will find techniques in the Annotated Teacher's Edition of *C'est à toi!* that will help them in the process.

Philosophy and Learning Strategies

C'est à toi! is a function-based textbook series that uses a communicative approach to teach students the French language within the context of the francophone world. Students acquire proficiency in listening to, speaking, reading and writing French while developing cultural sensitivity to the every-day activities of French-speaking people throughout the world. Since the focus of the classroom is student interaction, from day one students practice communicating easily and confidently with their peers in paired or cooperative learning groups. A balance of activities, both in the textbook and in the comprehensive ancillary program, allows students with a variety of learning styles to be success-ful in French as they progress from carefully structured practice to more creative expression. The five "Cs" addressed in *Standards for Foreign Language Learning: Preparing for the 21st Century* are artfully interwoven throughout each section of the textbook, integrating the principles of COMMUNICATION, CULTURES, CONNECTIONS, COMPARISONS and COMMUNITIES to help prepare students for an active, informed role as world citizens in the new millennium.

Many activities in the student textbook, as well as additional activities suggested in the color-coded sections of the Annotated Teacher's Edition, incorporate the following learning strategies and techniques to make learning more actively student centered and relevant to those with diverse learning styles.

- **Paired Activities**

  As the teacher-centered classroom moves toward the student-centered classroom where students are directly involved in and responsible for their own learning, teachers find that paired activities (in which one student is paired with a partner):
  1. give students markedly increased practice time in using French
  2. promote cooperation with others to achieve clearly stated goals
  3. instill in students greater self-confidence in their language abilities by placing them with their peers in less-threatening situations
  4. place students in more realistic, communicative settings
  5. lead to increased student involvement and motivation
  6. provide for a variation in classroom routine
  7. allow the teacher to assume a facilitating role, circulating throughout the room to answer questions and assist those who can benefit from individual help

  In order to assure students' success in a paired activity, teachers should make certain that the activity's goal is clearly communicated to students, tell them how to proceed in order to achieve their goal (provide a model), announce how much time they have to finish their task and inform them how their learning will be evaluated at the end of the activity. Paired activities appear in the **Pratique**, **Communication** and **C'est à moi!** sections of the textbook as well as in the color-coded Paired Practice section of the Annotated Teacher's Edition.

- **Cooperative Group Activities**

  Cooperative learning involves students working together to access, share and process knowledge, increase academic competencies and develop interpersonal and small group social skills. Putting students in cooperative learning groups makes them individually accountable for the outcome of their learning. Each member of a cooperative group must assume some responsibility for completing his or her task in order for the group to attain the stated goal. Students practice positive interdependence as they interact face-to-face with each other. Usually cooperative learning groups consist of four students who are grouped heterogeneously. As with paired activities, the teacher's role is to clearly communicate the activity's goal, tell how to proceed, set time limits and clarify evaluation procedures. When assigning group roles, the teacher should divide up responsibilities to ensure students' interdependence and cooperation. Each group should have a leader or facilitator, recorder and reporter. The final step in a cooperative group activity is to share the group's product with the rest of the class, who, along with the teacher, should assess the quality of the group's production. Cooperative learning activities are provided in the **Communication** and **C'est à moi!** sections of the textbook as well as in the color-coded Cooperative Group Practice section of the Annotated Teacher's Edition.

- **TPR Activities**

In the TPR (Total Physical Response) approach to second language acquisition, students are actively engaged in listening comprehension activities while limiting their responses to physical rather than to verbal demonstrations of comprehension. The teacher initially gives commands or verbal cues that elicit specific student behavior. Students may respond, for example, by pointing, gesturing, moving around the classroom or manipulating objects. This is an effective method of introducing new vocabulary words and expressions as well as new structures. This physical response to verbal stimuli aids students' comprehension of new elements and helps students to internalize and remember them longer. A list of practical classroom commands (**Expressions de communication**) that are useful in doing TPR activities is located on page TE42 of the Annotated Teacher's Edition. There are TPR activities in the color-coded TPR and Games sections of the Annotated Teacher's Edition.

- **Connections Activities (Cross-curricular)**

The French language and francophone culture are artfully interwoven into other areas of the secondary school curriculum so that students form connections to additional bodies of knowledge that may be unavailable to the monolingual English speaker. For example, students use their knowledge of French language and francophone culture as a stepping stone to a deeper understanding of geography, history, mathematics, art, music and science. Cross-curricular activities help to expand students' global thinking and understanding as enlightened world citizens. Connections activities are found in the **Pratique** and **Communication** sections of the textbook as well as in the color-coded Connections section of the Annotated Teacher's Edition.

- **Comparisons Activities (Critical Thinking)**

It is essential to emphasize the development of critical thinking skills, or higher order thinking skills, if our students are to succeed in school and later in life. There are many activities in *C'est à toi!* in which students practice comparing French with English and critical thinking. The cognitive abilities and their associated critical thinking skills included in the program are: knowledge acquisition (locate, describe, identify, list, match, name); comprehension (summarize, rewrite, rearrange, paraphrase); analysis (compare and contrast, order, categorize, distinguish); evaluation (conclude, justify); synthesis (associate, combine, compile, plan, generalize); and application (compose, create, design, produce). Comparisons activities appear in both the **Pratique** and **Communication** sections of the textbook and in the color-coded Comparisons section of the Annotated Teachers' Edition.

- **Activities to Engage Students' Multiple Intelligences**

  Many factors affect learning. For years teachers have recognized that students' intelligence, social environment and motivation all need to be considered. In addition, not all students learn the same way. Students' diverse learning styles need to be addressed in different ways in order to maximize individual potential.

  Recent explorations in how the brain works and human intelligence have provided a wealth of valuable information that is changing the perspectives of learning and teaching. Howard Gardner's Multiple Intelligences Theory proposes a pluralized way of understanding the intellect. It states that people have varying abilities in many different areas of thought and learning, and these abilities affect people's interests and how quickly they assimilate new information and skills. Gardner says that our brain processes and uses information either separately or together in concert through eight different intelligences: verbal-linguistic, logical-mathematical, visual-spatial, bodily kinesthetic, musical-rhythmic, interpersonal, intrapersonal and naturalist. The general characteristics associated with each of these intelligences are described below along with suggested instructional strategies.

  Verbal-Linguistic: These students demonstrate a strong appreciation for and fascination with words and language. People who display verbal-linguistic intelligence enjoy writing, reading, word searches, crossword puzzles and storytelling.

  Teaching Strategies:
  Tell a story.
  Summarize a magazine or newspaper article.
  Write a poem.
  Discuss the meaning of a song.
  Write to a keypal on the Internet.

  Logical-Mathematical: These students like establishing patterns and categorizing words and symbols. Students with logical-mathematical intelligence enjoy mathematics, experiments and games that involve strategy or rational thought.

  Teaching Strategies:
  Calculate the temperature in degrees Celsius.
  Double or triple a recipe.
  Write an analysis of an event.
  List the reasons why something happened.
  Tabulate the total cost of a shopping trip.

  Visual-Spatial: These students think in pictures and can conceptualize well. They often like complicated puzzles and may be seen drawing a picture, doodling, constructing something from the objects that surround them or daydreaming. They are able to imagine how something would look from a verbal description.

  Teaching Strategies:
  Write a summary comparing the artistic styles of two paintings.
  Draw the ideal house.
  Design a theme park.
  Identify a shape based on a classmate's description.
  Do a creative presentation using video and slides.

Bodily-Kinesthetic: Students who are athletic may demonstrate bodily-kinesthetic intelligence. They learn best by doing what they enjoy and want to learn through movement and touch. They express their thoughts with body movement. They are good with hands-on activities, such as sewing, woodworking, dancing, athletics and crafts.

Teaching Strategies:
Perform a dance from a francophone country.
Act out a part from a play.
Build a housing structure that is reminiscent of one that appears in the textbook.
Perform an activity as directed by a classmate or the teacher (TPR).
Create artwork that represents some aspect of the francophone world.

Musical-Rhythmic: These students can be observed singing or tapping out a tune on a desk or other nearby object. They are discriminating listeners who can hear a song once and then are able to play or sing the tune. Students who demonstrate musical intelligence catch what is said the first time, whereas others around them may need to hear the same thing repeated a number of times.

Teaching Strategies:
Write a song.
Listen to and describe a musical piece.
Perform a song.
Identify musical styles of several musicians from the francophone world.
Prepare a comparison of the music of two or more musicians.

Interpersonal: Students with interpersonal intelligence are natural leaders. They communicate well, empathize with others and often know what someone is thinking or feeling without having to hear the person speak.

Teaching Strategies:
Role-play a vendor making a sale.
Lead a discussion.
Debate an issue.
Organize and direct a poll.
Negotiate a settlement.

Intrapersonal: People with intrapersonal intelligence may appear to be shy. They are self-motivated and are very aware of their own thoughts and feelings about a given subject.

Teaching Strategies:
Write answers to questions about personal life.
Prepare a written plan for a career path.
Determine the pros and cons of an issue.
Create a list of favorite activities.
Write a poem expressing feelings.

Naturalist: Students with naturalist intelligence might have a special ability to observe, understand and apply learning to the natural environment. For example, students with naturalist intelligence may collect data about the environmental conditions for a particular place and instinctively know what crop would grow best there.

Teaching Strategies:
Draw or photograph and then present to the class an object found in nature.
Collect and categorize objects from the natural world.
Do research and present findings about a wildlife protection project.
Keep a notebook of observations of nature.
Go on a nature hike or field trip.

It is important to understand that these intelligences exist in everyone in different degrees and in different combinations. These intelligences do not relate specifically to content areas, but rather to the ability to process information. The Multiple Intelligences Theory reflects a way of thinking about people that not only allows for similarities, but also for differences. It fosters inclusion, increases opportunities for enrichment, builds self-esteem and develops respect for individuals and the gifts they bring to the classroom. In a setting that fosters the multiple intelligences, all students are allowed to learn through their strengths and to share their expertise with others.

Weaving the magic of the diversity of learning with the intent of "intelligence fair" strategies challenges all teachers to explore new possibilities to honor human potential. There are activities to engage students' multiple intelligences in the **Communication** and **C'est à moi!** sections of the textbook as well as in the color-coded Teacher's Notes and Connections sections of the Annotated Teacher's Edition.

- **Games**

Games in French are excellent motivational tools that give students the opportunity to learn in a context that varies from the daily routine. During this "learning pause," students review and reinforce previously introduced material as they expand on their language skills. French songs are also presented in the color-coded Games section of the Annotated Teacher's Edition.

Model Lesson Plans

Because instructional approaches and the length of class periods vary greatly among teachers and schools, it is difficult to provide a detailed plan for each individual lesson that would apply to all students using *C'est à toi!* Many school districts offer traditional 45- to 55-minute daily class periods. Other districts have implemented a block scheduling system in which class periods range from 75 to 110 minutes. These block schedules may involve consecutive days for a whole semester, alternate days for a year or other variations.

In these model lesson plans we offer some suggested guidelines for the effective use of the materials in **Unité 2**. The first schedule suggests how the textbook might be used in a traditional 50-minute class period. In this case, 18 days are allotted for each **unité** plus assessment. Assuming 180 days of 50-minute class periods, the third-level textbook can be covered entirely in one year at the high school level.

The second schedule demonstrates how you might use the textbook in a 4/4 semester block scheduling plan. In this case, nine days are allotted for each **unité** plus assessment. Assuming 90 days of 90-minute class periods, the third-level textbook can be covered entirely in one year at the high school level.

To see lesson plans for each **unité** in the *C'est à toi!* program, consult the Program Manager with Daily Lesson Plans.

Model Unit (*Unité 2*)
Traditional Class Period (50 minutes)

Day 1 — *Leçon A*

Textbook	Ancillary materials/activities
1. Warm-up: Review *passé composé* and vocabulary from *Unité 1*	
2. *Dossier ouvert,* p. 54	
3. *Tes empreintes ici,* p. 54	ATE: Comparisons, p. 56
4. Introduce the functions for *Leçon A* and vocabulary, pp. 54-55	Audiocassette/CD: Adjectives (Side A, Track 1)
5. *Dialogue,* pp. 56-57	Audiocassette/CD: *Dialogue* (Side A, Track 2) Workbook Activity 2, pp. 40-41
6. *Activité* 1, pp. 57-58	

Day 2 — *Leçon A*

Textbook	Ancillary materials/activities
1. Warm-up: Review vocabulary, p. 55	Workbook Activity 1, pp. 39-40
2. *Activités* 2-3, p. 58	Audiocassette/CD: Activity 3 (Side A, Track 3) ATE: Paired Practice, p. 58
3. *Enquête culturelle,* pp. 59-61	Workbook Activity 3, p. 42 ATE: Comparisons, p. 60
4. *Activités* 4-5, pp. 62-63	ATE: TPR, p. 63

Day 3 — *Leçon A*
Textbook

1. Warm-up: Review *Dialogue*, pp. 56-57

2. *Communication électronique*, p. 96

3. *Journal personnel,* p. 64

4. Imperfect tense, pp. 64-65

5. *Activités* 6-8, pp. 65-66

Ancillary materials/activities

Workbook Activity 4, pp. 42-43
ATE: Comparisons, p. 64
ATE: Cooperative Group Practice, p. 65

Audiocassette/CD: Activity 6 (Side A, Track 4)

Day 4 — *Leçon A*
Textbook

1. Warm-up: Review imperfect tense

2. Present participle, pp. 67-68

3. *Pratique* 9-11, pp. 68-69

Ancillary materials/activities

Workbook Activity 5, pp. 43-44
ATE: Game *(La tempête)*, p. 95

Workbook Activity 6, pp. 45-46
ATE: TPR, p. 67
ATE: Cooperative Group Practice, p. 68

Audiocassette/CD: Activities 10-11 (Side A, Tracks 5-6)

Day 5 — *Leçon A*
Textbook

1. Warm-up: Review present participle

2. *Communication* 12-14, pp. 70-71

3. *Sur la bonne piste,* pp. 71-72

4. *Activité* 15, p. 72

Ancillary materials/activities

ATE: Game (Sentence Match), p. 95
ATE: Paired Practice, p. 69

ATE: Paired Practice, p. 70

Workbook Activity 7, pp. 46-48
ATE: Cooperative Group Practice, p. 71

Day 6 — *Leçons A/B*
Textbook

1. Warm-up: Review all of *Leçon A* for quiz

2. Quiz *Leçon A,* pp. 10-12

3. Introduce the functions for *Leçon B* and vocabulary, p. 73

Ancillary materials/activities

Listening Activity 1, p. SA3

Quiz *Leçon A,* pp. 10-12

Audiocassette/CD: Office Workers and Reflexive Verbs (Side B, Track 7)

Day 7 — *Leçon B*
Textbook

1. Warm-up: Review vocabulary, p. 73

Ancillary materials/activities

Workbook Activity 8, p. 49

2. *La lettre*, pp. 74-75	Audiocassette/CD: *La lettre* (Side B, Track 8) Transparency 10
3. *Activités* 1-3, p. 76	Audiocassette/CD: Activities 1 and 3 (Side B, Tracks 9-10)

Day 8 — *Leçon B*
Textbook   **Ancillary materials/activities**

1. Warm-up: Review *La lettre,* pp. 74-75	Workbook Activity 9, p. 50 ATE: Game, p. 76
2. *Enquête culturelle,* pp. 77-78	Transparency 11
3. *Activité* 4, p. 78	

Day 9 — *Leçon B*
Textbook   **Ancillary materials/activities**

1. Warm-up: Review *Enquête culturelle*	Workbook Activity 10, p. 51
2. *Journal personnel,* p. 79	
3. Reflexive verbs, pp. 79-80	Workbook Activity 11, pp. 51-52 ATE: Comparisons, p. 79
4. *Pratique* 5-8, pp. 80-81	Audiocassette/CD: Activities 5-6 (Side B, Tracks 11-12)

Day 10 — *Leçon B*
Textbook   **Ancillary materials/activities**

1. Warm-up: Review reflexive verbs	ATE: Cooperative Group Practice, p. 81 Workbook Activity 12, p. 52
2. Negation, p. 82	ATE: Comparisons, p. 82
3. *Pratique* 9-11, pp. 82-83	Audiocassette/CD: Activity 9 (Side B, Track 13)

Day 11 — *Leçon B*
Textbook   **Ancillary materials/activities**

1. Warm-up: Review negation	Workbook Activity 13, pp. 53-54
2. Other negative expressions, pp. 83-84	Workbook Activity 14, pp. 54-55 ATE: Cooperative Group Practice, p. 86 ATE: Paired Practice, p. 87
3. *Pratique* 12-13, pp. 85-86	Audiocassette/CD: Activities 12-13 (Side B, Tracks 14-15)

Day 12 — *Leçon B*
Textbook   **Ancillary materials/activities**

1. Warm-up: Review other negative expressions	ATE: Paired Practice, p. 85 Workbook Activity 15, pp. 55-56

2. *Pratique* 14-15, pp. 86-87

Audiocassette/CD: Activities 14-15 (Side B, Tracks 16-17)

3. *Communication* 16-17, pp. 87-88

Day 13 — *Leçon B*
Textbook

Ancillary materials/activities

1. Warm-up: Review all of *Leçon B* for quiz

Listening Activity 2, p. SA3

2. Quiz *Leçon B,* pp. 13-16

Quiz *Leçon B,* pp. 13-16

3. *Sur la bonne piste,* p. 88

Day 14 — *Leçon B*
Textbook

Ancillary materials/activities

1. Warm-up: *Dossier fermé,* p. 91

2. *Activité* 18, p. 88

3. *Déjeuner du matin,* pp. 88-89

Audiocassette/CD: *Sur la bonne piste—Déjeuner du matin* (Side B, Track 18)

4. *Activité* 19, p. 89

Day 15 — *Leçon C*
Textbook

Ancillary materials/activities

1. Warm-up: Review *Déjeuner du matin*

2. *Activités* 20-22, pp. 89-90

Audiocassette/CD: *Sur la bonne piste—Le Cancre* (Side B, Track 19)

3. *Le Cancre,* p. 90

Day 16 — *Leçon B*
Textbook

Ancillary materials/activities

1. Warm-up: Review *Le Cancre*

2. *Activités* 23-26, p. 91

ATE: Comparisons, p. 91

Day 17 — *Leçon B*
Textbook

Ancillary materials/activities

1. Warm-up: *C'est à moi!,* p. 92

2. *Communication orale,* p. 93

3. *Communication écrite,* p. 94

ATE: Dictation, p. 94

4. *À moi de jouer!,* p. 96

Day 18 — Assessment
Textbook

Ancillary materials/activities

1. Warm-up: *Communication active,* pp. 94-95

Listening Activity 3, pp. SA3-4

2. Review highlights of unit

3. *Unité 2* test   Unit Tests Booklet, Unit Tests Video, Unit Tests Audiocassette/CD

Model Unit *(Unité 2)*
Block Scheduling (90 minutes)

Day 1 — *Leçon A*
Textbook

Textbook	Ancillary materials/activities
1. Warm-up: Review *passé composé* and vocabulary from *Unité* 1	
2. *Dossier ouvert,* p. 54	
3. *Tes empreintes ici,* p. 54	ATE: Comparisons, p. 56
4. Introduce the functions for *Leçon A* and vocabulary, pp. 54-55	Audiocassette/CD: Adjectives (Side A, Track 1) Workbook Activity 1, pp. 39-40
5. *Dialogue,* pp. 56-57	Audiocassette/CD: *Dialogue* (Side A, Track 2)
6. *Activités* 1-3, pp. 57-58	Audiocassette/CD: Activity 3 (Side A, Track 3) ATE: Paired Practice, p. 58
7. *Enquête culturelle,* pp. 59-61	Workbook Activity 3, p. 42 ATE: Comparisons, p. 60
8. *Activités* 4-5, pp. 62-63	ATE: TPR, p. 63

Day 2 — *Leçon A*
Textbook

Textbook	Ancillary materials/activities
1. Warm-up: Review *Dialogue,* pp. 56-57	Workbook Activity 2, pp. 40-41
2. *Journal personnel,* p. 64	
3. Imperfect tense, pp. 64-65	Workbook Activity 4, pp. 42-43 ATE: Comparisons, p. 64 ATE: Cooperative Group Practice, p. 65
4. *Activités* 6-8, pp. 65-66	Audiocassette/CD: Activity 6 (Side A, Track 4)
5. Present participle, pp. 67-68	Workbook Activity 6, pp. 45-46 ATE: TPR, p. 67 ATE: Paired Practice, p. 69 ATE: Cooperative Group Practice, p. 68 ATE: Game (Sentence Match), p. 95
6. *Pratique* 9-11, pp. 68-69	Audiocassette/CD: Activities 10-11 (Side A, Tracks 5-6)

Day 3 — *Leçons A/B*
Textbook

Ancillary materials/activities	

1. Warm-up: Review imperfect tense

   ATE: Game (*La tempête*), p. 95
   Workbook Activity 5, pp. 43-44

2. *Communication* 12-14, pp. 70-71

   ATE: Paired Practice, p. 70

3. *Sur la bonne piste,* pp. 71-72

   Workbook Activity 7, pp. 46-48
   ATE: Cooperative Group Practice, p. 71

4. *Activité* 15, p. 72

5. Review all of *Leçon A* for quiz

   Listening Activity 1, p. SA3

6. Quiz *Leçon A,* pp. 10-12

   Quiz *Leçon A,* pp. 10-12

7. Introduce the functions for *Leçon B* and vocabulary, p. 73

   Audiocassette/CD: Office Workers and Reflexive Verbs (Side B, Track 7)

Day 4 — *Leçon B*
Textbook

Ancillary materials/activities

1. Warm-up: Review vocabulary, p. 73

   Workbook Activity 8, p. 49

2. *La lettre,* pp. 74-75

   Audiocassette/CD: *La lettre* (Side B, Track 8)
   Workbook Activity 9, p. 50
   Transparency 10
   ATE: Game, p. 76

3. *Activités* 1-3, p. 76

   Audiocassette/CD: Activities 1 and 3 (Side B, Tracks 9-10)

4. *Enquête culturelle,* pp. 77-78

   Workbook Activity 10, p. 51
   Transparency 11

5. *Activité* 4, p. 78

6. *Journal personnel,* p. 79

7. Reflexive verbs, pp. 79-80

   Workbook Activity 11, pp. 51-52
   ATE: Comparisons, p. 79

8. *Pratique* 5-8, pp. 80-81

   Audiocassette/CD: Activities 5-6 (Side B, Tracks 11-12)

Day 5 — *Leçon B*
Textbook

Ancillary materials/activities

1. Warm-up: Review reflexive verbs

   ATE: Cooperative Group Practice, p. 81
   Workbook Activity 12, p. 52

2. Negation, p. 82

   Workbook Activity 13, pp. 53-54
   ATE: Comparisons, p. 82

3. *Pratique* 9-11, pp. 82-83

   Audiocassette/CD: Activity 9 (Side B, Track 13)

Textbook	Ancillary materials/activities
4. Other negative expressions, pp. 83-84	Workbook Activity 14, pp. 54-55 ATE: Cooperative Group Practice, p. 86 ATE: Paired Practice, p. 87
5. *Pratique* 12-13, pp. 85-86	Audiocassette/CD: Activities 12-13 (Side B, Tracks 14-15)

Day 6 — *Leçon B*

Textbook	Ancillary materials/activities
1. Warm-up: Review other negative expressions	ATE: Paired Practice, p. 85 Workbook Activity 15, pp. 55-56
2. *Pratique* 14-15, pp. 86-87	Audiocassette/CD: Activities 14-15 (Side B, Tracks 16-17)
3. *Communication* 16-17, pp. 87-88	
4. Review all of *Leçon B* for quiz	Listening Activity 2, p. SA3
5. Quiz *Leçon B,* pp. 13-16	Quiz *Leçon B,* pp. 13-16
6. *Sur la bonne piste*, p. 88	
7. *Activité* 18, p. 88	
8. *Déjeuner du matin*, pp. 88-89	Audiocassette/CD: *Sur la bonne piste—Déjeuner du matin* (Side B, Track 18)
9. *Activité* 19, p. 89	

Day 7 — *Leçon B*

Textbook	Ancillary materials/activities
1. Warm-up: Review *Déjeuner du matin*	
2. *Activités* 20-22, pp. 89-90	
3. *Le Cancre*, p. 90	Audiocassette/CD: *Sur la bonne piste—Le Cancre* (Side B, Track 19) ATE: Comparisons, p. 91
4. *Activité* 23, p. 91	

Day 8 — *Leçon B*

Textbook	Ancillary materials/activities
1. Warm-up: Review *Le Cancre*	
2. *Activités* 24-26, p. 91	
3. *Dossier fermé*, p. 91	
4. *C'est à moi!*, p. 92	
5. *Communication orale*, p. 93	

6. *Communication écrite*, p. 94   ATE: Dictation, p. 94

7. *À moi de jouer!*, p. 96

Day 9 — Assessment
Textbook   ## Ancillary materials/activities

1. Warm-up: *Communication active*, pp. 94-95   Listening Activity 3, pp. SA3-4

2. Review highlights of unit

3. *Unité 2* test   Unit Tests Booklet, Unit Tests Video, Unit Tests
                                                Audiocassette/CD

EXPRESSIONS DE COMMUNICATION

À demain.	*See you tomorrow.*
Allez au laboratoire.	*Go to the laboratory.*
Allez au tableau.	*Go to the board.*
Attention.	*Be careful.*
Bon appétit.	*Have a good meal.*
Bon weekend.	*Have a good weekend.*
Bonne journée.	*Have a good day.*
C'est bien.	*That's good.*
Comment dit-on...?	*How do you say . . . ?*
Comment s'appelle-t-il?	*What's his name?*
Comment s'appelle-t-elle?	*What's her name?*
Continuons.	*Let's continue.*
Écoutez.	*Listen.*
Écrivez.	*Write.*
Encore.	*Again.*
Épelez.	*Spell.*
Fermez la porte.	*Close the door.*
Fermez le livre.	*Close your books.*
Je ne comprends pas.	*I don't understand.*
Lisez.	*Read.*
Maintenant, une dictée.	*And now a dictation.*
Montrez-moi....	*Show me . . . .*
Ouvrez la porte.	*Open the door.*
Ouvrez le livre à la page....	*Open your book to page . . . .*
Prenez votre (vos) livre(s).	*Take out your book(s).*
Présentez-moi....	*Introduce me . . . .*
Présentez-nous....	*Introduce us . . . .*
Répétez.	*Repeat.*
Répondez.	*Answer.*
Tous ensemble.	*All together.*

Functions

in *C'est à toi!*

The number following the communicative function indicates in what unit a specific way to express that function is presented for the first time.

accept and refuse an invitation 10
admit 5, 10
agree and disagree 5, 10
apologize 2
ask about importance and unimportance 3
ask about preference 7
ask for a price 10
ask for help 10
ask for information 2, 6, 7
ask for permission 10
ask what something is 9

boast 8, 9

clarify 7
compare 3, 7, 9, 10
confirm a known fact 1
congratulate and commiserate 6
control the volume of a conversation 5

describe character 7, 8, 10
describe how things were 2
describe past events 1, 8, 9, 10
describe people you remember 5
describe physical traits 2
describe talents and abilities 4
describe temperament 2

estimate 10
evaluate 4
explain a problem 4
explain something 1, 2, 6, 7, 8
express agreement and disagreement 7
express appreciation 4, 6, 8
express astonishment and disbelief 1, 2
express certainty and uncertainty 4
express compassion 7
express complaints 5
express concern 2
express confirmation 10
express criticism 8
express desire 1, 4
express disagreement 4
express disappointment 9, 10
express displeasure 10
express dissatisfaction 5
express emotions 1, 2, 10
express enthusiasm 1, 6, 9
express fear 5
express gratitude 10
express happiness 5
express hope 4
express importance and unimportance 3, 7
express inability 1
express incapability 8
express indifference 9
express intentions 4
express likes and dislikes 3, 5